COLOMBIA

100+ Amazing & Interesting Facts You Didn't know Before

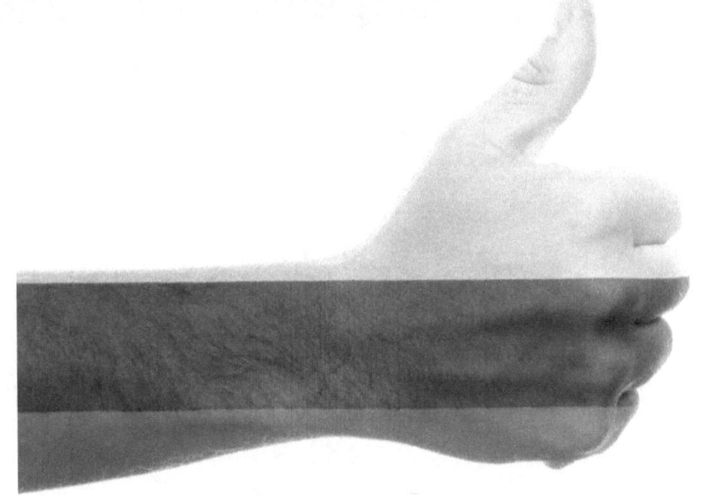

BANDANA OJHA

<u>Introduction</u>

Filled with up-to-date information, fascinating & fun facts this book **COLOMBIA: 100+ Amazing & Interesting Facts You Didn't Know Before"** is the best book for kids to find out more about "The gateway to South America". This book would satisfy the children's curiosity and help them to understand why Colombia attracts millions of visitors annually and what makes it different from other South American Countries. This book gives a story, history & explores the country's best cuisine, architecture, fashion, art, language, people, places, national symbols, and many more. It is a fun and fascinating way for young readers to find out more interesting facts. This is a great chance for every kid to expand their knowledge about Colombia and impress family and friends with all "discovered and never knew before" amazing facts.

Colombia, officially Republic of Colombia, is a country of northwestern South America.

It is bordered by the Caribbean Sea to the north, Venezuela to the east, Brazil to the southeast, Ecuador and Peru to the south, the Pacific Ocean to the west, and Panama to the northwest.

It is the only country in South America with coastlines and islands along both Atlantic and Pacific oceans.

Colombia is named after the legendary Italian explorer, navigator, and colonizer – Christopher Columbus.

Colombia is the 25th Largest Country on Earth. It is more than twice the size of France or Spain and has the same length of coastline as the U.S. pacific coast.

Colombia is nicknamed the "gateway to South America" because it sits in the northwestern part of the continent where South America connects with Central and North America.

Colombia has been inhabited by various indigenous peoples since at least 12,000 BCE, including the Muisca, Quimbaya, and the Tairona.

The Spanish landed first in La Guajira in 1499 and by the mid-16th century colonized parts of the region, establishing the New Kingdom of Granada, with Santa Fé de Bogotá as its capital.

Independence from the Spanish Empire was achieved in 1819, with what is now Colombia emerging as the United Provinces of New Granada.

The Republic of Colombia was finally declared in 1886

National Day of Colombia is 20th

National founder of Colombia
is Simón Bolívar.

National hero
of Colombia is
Antonio Narino.

National Motto of Colombia is "Libertad y Orden" ("Liberty and Order").

National Flag is "The Flag of Colombia

The National Flag of Colombia was officially adopted on November 26, 1861.

The flag was designed by Francisco de Miranda – a Venezuelan General.

The Flag features three horizontal bands of yellow (top, double width), blue, and red.

The colors of the flag are commonly interpreted in two ways. One version indicates that the yellow symbolizes sovereignty and justice, blue as loyalty and vigilance, and red represents the valor shown and the victory achieved during the battles for independence from Spain.

Another version claims that yellow represents the gold Colombia once owned until the arrival of the Spanish, blue indicates the country's contact with two oceans and red represents the blood that Colombians spent in their struggle for independence from Spain.

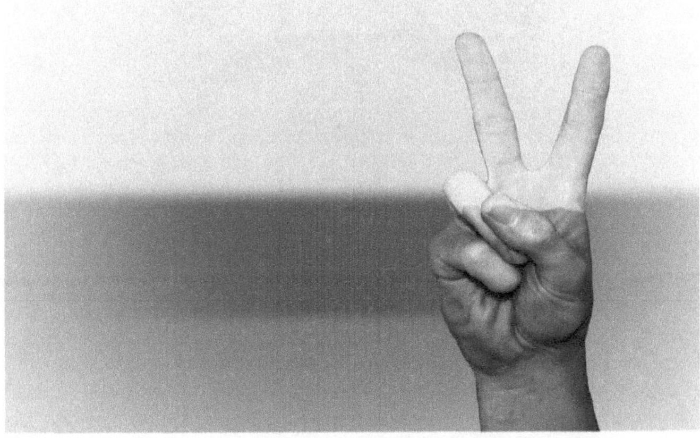

The flag has a width-to-length proportion ratio of 2:3.

The national emblem is the "The National Coat of Arms of Colombia."

LIBERTAD Y ORDEN

The current Coat of Arms of Colombia was officially adopted on May 9, 1834.

At the center of the Coat of Arms is a shield which is divided into three sections. the base section shows the Isthmus of Panama, which belonged to Colombia until 1903. The middle section uses a Phrygian cap, which is a traditional symbol of freedom. The top section shows a pomegranate with two cornucopias (horn of plenty), which is a colonial symbol for the Viceroyalty of New Grenada. At the top of the shield is an endangered species – the Andean Condor, holding an olive branch in its beak. Behind the shield is a sail made from the Colombian National Flag, draped over the spears. Above the shield is a ribbon displaying the national motto: "Libertad Y Orden".

"Himno Nacional de la República de Colombia" is the national anthem of the Republic of Colombia.

The music of the anthem was composed by an Italian Opera singer named Oreste Sindici and the lyrics have been written by former Colombian President - Rafael Núnez.

The anthem was officially adopted on October 28, 1920.

The official currency of Colombia is the Colombian peso (COL$).

National dish of Colombia is Bandeja Paisa

Bandeja Paisa consists of rice, plantain, arepa (corn cakes), avocado, minced meat, chorizo, black sausage, and fried pork rind. There's also a fried egg thrown on top for good measure.

Breakfast is an important meal in Colombia. Lunch, however, is a serious affair. Most Colombians take a two-hour lunch break each day. For many Colombians, dinner is the least important meal of the day.

National bird of Colombia is Andean Condor.

Andean condor is one of the world's largest birds, a vulture with a wingspan of more than three meters. It is also one of the world's longest living birds, often surpassing 70 years of age.

The Andean Condor symbolizes the Colombian people's freedom and sovereignty. It was selected as a national symbol in 1834. Unfortunately, it is considered a near threatened species by the International Union for the Conservation of Nature -IUCN.

Colombians are the best dancers in South America!

The cattleya trianae orchid, commonly known as "May flower" or "May lily" has been the national flower of Colombia since 1936

There are more than 4,000 orchid species in the country. Therefore, it's called the **Orchid Capital of the world.** Southeast Asia comes in next with over 1,500 wild orchid species.

The orchid was chosen because the lower part of its flower can appear yellow, blue, and red – the colors of the Colombian flag.

The national drink of Colombia is Aguardiente or Guaro.

Aguardiente, or firewater, is a liquor made from sugar cane and anise. It is most often enjoyed at celebrations. By adding different amounts of aniseed, different flavors are obtained

National color(s) of Colombia is Yellow, Blue and Red.

National tree of Colombia is
the wax palm tree.

National sports of Colombia is Tejo
(TAY-HO).

Tejo is one of the country's oldest and possibly the most popular sport in Colombia. It is originated in indigenous groups around 500 years ago.

The most popular sport in Colombia is football (soccer). The Colombian national team won the 2001 Copa América (South American Championship).

Other popular and successful sports of Colombia include roller-skating, weightlifting, baseball, boxing, motorsport and cycling.

National Museum of Colombia is "Colombian National Museum."

The National Museum is the oldest in the country and one of the oldest in the continent, built in 1823. Its fortress architecture is built in stone and brick.

The museum houses a collection of over 20,000 pieces including works of art and objects representing different national history periods.

National poet of Colombia is José Asunción Silva.

National mausoleum of Colombia is Panteon De Los Proceres.

National archive of Colombia is
General National Archive.

General National Archive
headquarter is located in the city
of Bogotá and was designed by
the architect Rogelio Salmona.

National Museum of Colombia is
"Colombian National Museum."

National language of Colombia is Spanish. More than 99.5% of Colombians speak Spanish.

National airline of Colombia is Avianca.

Avianca is the largest airline in Colombia and second largest in Latin America, after LATAM of Chile.

Highest Peak of Colombia is Pico
Cristóbal Colón, with an estimated
height of 5,730 meters (18,800 ft).

The peak is named after Christopher
Columbus.

There is a permanent snowcap on
this peak and it is the part of
the Sierra Nevada de Santa
Marta range.

Colombia's Sierra Nevada de Santa Marta, at 13,000 m, is the world's highest coastal mountain range.

Colombia's capital city is Bogotá. It is the financial and commercial heart of Colombia, with the most business activity and is the leading destination for new foreign direct investment projects coming into Latin America and Colombia

Before the Spanish rule arrived, Bogota, was founded by the Muisca community. They created a settlement that was then referred as Bacata which means 'The Lady of the Andes' in Chibcha language. When the Spanish colonizers came, the area developed into the capital of the Empire.

The city is in the center of Colombia, on a high plateau known as the Bogotá savanna located in the Eastern Cordillera of the Andes. Bogotá is the third-highest capital in South America and in the world after Quito and La Paz, at an average of 2,640 meters (8,660 ft) above sea level.

National Hat of Colombia is Sombrero Vueltiao.

The sombrero vueltiao is a woven hat that can take up to a month to make. The name means "turned hat" and refers to the way the hat is woven.

Sombreros vueltiaos are made by the
Zenu indigenous people from a type
of cane, known as caña fleche. The
cane leaves are cut into strips and
dried until they turn white. The
darkest are then soaked in mud for
up to four days and dried until they
turn black. The most intricate
sombrero vueltiao requires 54 strips
and are so densely woven they can
be folded and put into a pocket
without being damaged.

Most of these handmade hats are
produced by entire Zenú families
located in the Departments
of Cordoba and Sucre.

The quality of the hat is
determined by the number of pairs
of fibers braided together to make
the hat, and its bending flexibility.
The more flexible the hat is, the
higher is its quality.

Tallest building of Colombia is Bd Bacatá Torre Sur. It is the sixth tallest building in South America.

BD Bacatá is the world's first crowdfunded skyscraper and the first skyscraper to be built in Colombia in 35 years. The structure is financed by over 3,800 Colombians.

The BD Bacatá was named after an old hotel which used to be in the construction site, but was sold to the Spanish design firm, Alonso Balaguer. The old hotel was demolished; however, its name will remain, as it acknowledges Bogotá's (and Colombia's) indigenous heritage.

Colombia's economy is the third largest in South America.

National instrument of Colombia is Colombian Tiple.

As a relative of the guitar the Colombian tiple is similar in appearance although slightly smaller (about 18%) than a standard classical guitar.

As with most chordophones of the guitar family, the Colombian tiple can be played either by strumming with the fingers or with a plectrum or a combination of both.

Colombian culture, architecture, food habits, language, and its constitution are all influenced by Spain.

The family is always the very center of the social structure of Colombian culture.

Columbia encompasses a variety of different landscapes including Amazon rainforest, mountains, deserts, and grasslands.

The town of Loro in Chaco experiences the most annual rainfall in the World. On average the rural town drowns in about 43 FEET of rainfall every year.

With an estimated 50 million people, Colombia is the third-most populous country in Latin America, after Brazil and Mexico.

Colombia's government is divided into three branches: the executive branch, headed by the President, the legislative branch, headed by the Congress and the judicial branch, headed by four high courts.

Colombia is the third largest exporter of coffee in the world after Brazil and Vietnam.

Ninety-five percent of the Colombian population are members of the Roman Catholic faith.

Colombia ranks first in the world for number of bird species with over 1,900 species of bird, more than Europe and North America combined.

Colombia has 10% of the world's mamals species, 14% of the amphibian species and 18% of the bird species of the world.

Colombia is the second most diverse country in the world for freshwater fish.

Colombia is second in the number of amphibian species and is the third most diverse country in reptiles and palms.

Colombia has the most endemic, or native species of butterfly in the world.

One of the rare species found in the vast ecosystem of Colombia is pink dolphins or Vaquitas.

The most important river system in Colombia is the Magdalena and it covers nearly a quarter of the surface of the entire country.

The Caño Cristales river, also referred to as the liquid rainbow, is 100km long. It changes its colors by the season. The colors range anywhere from shades of red, blue, and yellow, to orange, and green.

The vibrant water is unique and colors like this are not found in other streams on earth.

Colombia has a diverse range of climate zones, including tropical rainforests, savannas, steppes, deserts, and mountain climates.

Colombia is just a fun-loving country that celebrates 18 national holidays in a year. It comes second after India where most holidays are celebrated.

Colombians can use two surnames. They use both their paternal and maternal surnames.

The Xavier Pontifical University (1622) and the University of Santo Tomás (1580) are among the several excellent universities in Bogotá.

The International Center for Tropical Agriculture based in Colombia investigates the increasing challenge of global warming and food security.

During the colonial period, door knockers represent the homeowner's social status. Those with fish shapes are houses owned by sea merchants and sailors, lizards for aristocrats, and lions for those in the military.

70-90% of the world's emeralds come from Colombia! The Colombian emerald is highly esteemed in the gemstone world because of its deep bright green hue. It's the standard for quality gemstones.

Colombia has Coastline on Both the Caribbean and Pacific Ocean. It has two coastlines and many small coastal islands to the North and the West.

Colombia has 60 National Parks that cover over 10% of the Country.

One of the biggest national parks is the Unesco World Heritage Site of Chiribiquete National Park which is also known as, "The Maloca of the Jaguar". It spreads over 4.3 million hectares. This national park covers the Orinoquia, Guyana, Amazonia, and North Andes provinces.

La Chorrera is Colombia's highest multi-drop waterfall.

Colombia has the World's Tallest Palm Trees- the "Wax palms" which is native to the Cocora Valley's humid Andean forests.

The wax palm can reach 70 meters in height and can live up to 200 years.

A seedling takes around 50 years to reach the adult phase and each stem ring represents a year of growth.

Colombia has the world's largest flower festival in Medellin. It consists of flower exhibitions, a parade, and local flower growers who come together to share what they grow.

The flower festival celebrates Colombia's biodiversity and displays the most stunning flowers. During the festival, there are many other worthwhile events like an orchid expo, fireworks, art exhibitions, horse fairs, and more.

Colombia has been the world's second-largest exporter of wildflowers for more than 60 years, with most of its production happening in the central northwestern department of Antioquia. In the month of May 1957, Medellin's tourist bureau member, Arturo Uribe, suggested they host a "Fiesta de Flores" (Flower Party) in the city to celebrate Colombia's, and more specifically Antioquia's, success in exporting flowers to the world. That's how the flower festival started.

In 1958 Colombian doctor Alberto Vejarano Laverde and electrical engineer Jorge Reynolds Pombo constructed an external pacemaker which was successfully used to sustain a 70-year-old man. They are considered by many as the fathers of the life-saving pacemaker device.

Sophrology was invented by Professor Alfonso Caycedo, a Colombian neuropsychiatrist, in the 1960s, and describes the study of the consciousnes in harmony. It is widely practiced throughout Europe, and commonly used in sports, education, and social care, as it is thought to have a very positive impact on concentration, self-confidence, and energy levels.

Adriana Solano and Miguel Uribe, Colombian Industrial Designers are the creators of one of the most useful and innovative products for those who have lost their leg above the knee. It is a prosthesis that makes easier for them to climb or downstairs and allows them to bend their limb.

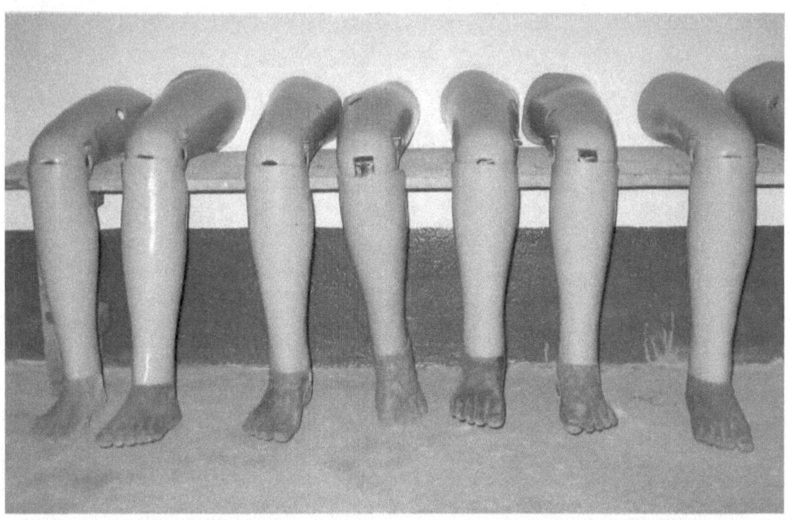

Colombia has the world's largest salsa festival known as Feria de Cali. It is held from December 25th to December 30th every year. This five-day festival contains grand musical, dance, and art performances.

The Carnival del Diablo, or Festival of the Devil, is held in the town of Rio Sucio. It features feasts, costumes, dancing, music, and poetry to ward off bad spirits.

It takes place every two years (in odd-numbered years) in early January. It is one of the best known and most popular carnivals in Colombia,

Cali, is the capital of the Valle del Cauca department, and the most populous city in southwest Colombia, is referred as the salsa capital of the world.

The city is very well known as "The Capital of the Plastic Surgeries" being a prime destination for people seeking cheap cosmetic surgery and aesthetician centers.

The Ibero-American Theater in Bogota hosts the world's largest art and cultural event in Colombia. Several theater groups and companies from all 5 continents come together to celebrate the festival.

Easter is the biggest festival of the year in Colombia. It is celebrated with a parade where people carry large wooden platforms depicting scenes from the bible through the streets.

Colombia is in the group of countries that are part of the Pacific Ring of Fire. This ring of fire has at least 452 volcanoes. Since Colombia's land is a part of it, this is prone to volcanic eruptions and earthquakes.

Colombians are extremely patriotic, and their laws reflect the same fact – 'Duty before life'. The mandatory law 198 of Colombia states that 'Oh Gloria immarcesible!' (O, Unfading Glory) should be played every day at 6 AM(when it gets light) and 6 PM (when it gets dark) on both radios and public television.

Please check this out:
Our other best-selling books for kids are-

All About **New York**: Interesting & Amazing Facts That Everyone Should Know

All About **New Jersey**: Interesting & Amazing Facts That Everyone Should Know

All About **Massachusetts**: 100+ Amazing Facts with Pictures

All About **Florida**: Interesting & Amazing Facts That Everyone Should Know

All About **California**: Interesting & Amazing Facts That Everyone Should Know

All About **Arizona**: Interesting & Amazing Facts That Everyone Should Know

All About **Texas**: Interesting & Amazing Facts That Everyone Should Know

All About **Minnesota**: Interesting & Amazing Facts That Everyone Should Know

All About **Illinois**: Interesting & Amazing Facts That Everyone Should Know

All About **New Mexico**: Interesting & Amazing Facts That Everyone Should Know

Know about Sharks: Interesting & Amazing Facts That Everyone Should Know

Please check this out:
Our other best-selling books for kids are-

Ukraine: Interesting & Amazing Facts That
Everyone Should Know

Germany: Interesting & Amazing Facts That
Everyone Should Know

Switzerland: Interesting & Amazing Facts That
Everyone Should Know

New Zealand: Interesting & Amazing Facts That
Everyone Should Know

Brazil: Interesting & Amazing Facts That
Everyone Should Know

Argentina: Interesting & Amazing Facts That
Everyone Should Know

Chile: Interesting & Amazing Facts That
Everyone Should Know

Denmark Interesting & Amazing Facts That
Everyone Should Know

All About **Canada**: Interesting & Amazing Facts That
Everyone Should Know

All About **Australia**: Interesting & Amazing Facts That
Everyone Should Know

All About **Italy**: Interesting & Amazing Facts That
Everyone Should Know

Please check this out:
Our other best-selling books for kids are-

All About **France**: Interesting & Amazing Facts That
Everyone Should Know

All About **Japan:** Interesting & Amazing Facts That
Everyone Should Know

Know About Whales: Interesting & Amazing Facts That
Everyone Should Know

Know About Dinosaurs: Interesting & Amazing Facts That
Everyone Should Know

Know About Kangaroos: Interesting & Amazing Facts That
Everyone Should Know

Know About Penguins: Interesting & Amazing Facts That
Everyone Should Know

Know About Dolphins :100 Interesting & Amazing Facts That Everyone Should Know

Know About Elephant: Interesting & Amazing Facts That
Everyone Should Know

Please check this out:
Our other best-selling books for kids
are-
100 Amazing Quiz Q & A About
Penguin: Never Known Before Penguin
Facts
Most Popular Animal Quiz book for Kids:
100 amazing animal facts
Quiz Book for Kids: Science, History,
Geography, Biology, Computer &
Information Technology
English Grammar for Kids: Most Easy Way
to learn English Grammar
Solar System & Space Science- Quiz for
Kids: What You Know About Solar System
English Grammar Practice Book for
elementary kids: 1000+ Practice
Questions with Answers

9 798223 383147